INTERNSHIP & VOLUNTEER OPPORTUNITIES

for People Who Love All Things Digital

Anastasia Suen

ROSEN
PUBLISHING®

New York

Pub. 25.00

Published in 2013 by The Rosen Publishing Group, Inc.
29 East 21st Street, New York, NY 10010

Copyright © 2013 by The Rosen Publishing Group, Inc.

First Edition

Library of Congress Cataloging-in-Publication Data

Suen, Anastasia.
Internship & volunteer opportunities for people who love all things digital/Anastasia Suen.
     p. cm.—(A foot in the door)
Includes bibliographical references and index.
ISBN 978-1-4488-8300-4 (library binding)
1. Computer science—Vocational guidance. 2. Internship programs.
3. Voluntarism. I. Title. II. Title: Internship and volunteer opportunities for people who love all things digital.
QA76.25.S83 2013
004.023—dc23

2012016456

Manufactured in the United States of America

CPSIA Compliance Information: Batch #W13YA: For further information, contact Rosen Publishing, New York, New York, at 1-800-237-9932.

Contents

For hundreds of years, apprentices learned new trades by working with older, more experienced people. Today, an apprentice is called an intern.

Introduction

Are you ready to be an apprentice? In the Middle Ages, it was common for a young person to study with an older person to learn a trade. This relationship was called an apprenticeship.

An apprenticeship provided benefits for both parties. The older person, called the master, shared his knowledge with a younger person who worked for him. In return, the apprentice learned how to do something new. Information was given in exchange for labor.

The apprentice worked with the master for several years. For his services, the apprentice learned a new trade and was provided for in other ways. The apprentice lived with the master and the other workers. He worked for his room and board, meals, and clothing. In other words, the master took the place of the apprentice's parents in providing for all of his needs.

Apprenticeships were set up not only to help someone learn a new trade but also to protect ideas and information. Knowing how to do something that others could not gave you an advantage. Learning a new skill was considered valuable and something to be protected. Only certain individuals were allowed to learn how to do the work for each trade.

Today, we have a new name for apprenticeships. We call them internships. An internship is a program that provides practical experience for beginners. An internship helps beginners learn a new profession. For a predetermined amount of time, a few hours a week or full-time for an entire summer, an intern works at a real company. Some internships are paid positions and some are not.

Today's internships teach you how to do the work for a new kind of trade. In this book we will talk about digital work: work that is done with computers. We'll explore the work done by photojournalists, camera operators, graphic designers, Web site designers, and social media managers. We'll also look at the work done by game testers, tech support, business systems managers, programmers, and app developers.

You don't need to move away from home to become an apprentice anymore. You can live at home and work as an intern part-time during the school year or full-time during the summer. The person you work for may or may not pay you for the work that you do. It is the skill and work experience that you're after. An internship during your college years can help you establish a foothold in a career after you graduate.

The best way to try out a career possibility in high school is to volunteer. When you volunteer, you agree to work for free. You give back to the community by helping others. You keep your skills sharp by using them in the service of others.

The work for a volunteer position can be ongoing. It doesn't always begin or end within a certain period of time like an internship does. This means you could volunteer throughout the year for a short period of time each week. You may find that this will fit into your schedule better. Volunteering is also an important addition to your college résumé and future job applications.

The other big difference between an internship and a volunteer position is that an internship is set up to teach you a new skill. A volunteer position, on the other hand, is all about what you can do for someone else. You will benefit because of what you learn during your experience, but a volunteer position is not always set up to train you. Learning a new skill may be up to you.

Chapter One

WHY INTERN OR VOLUNTEER?

If you could get a job that paid good money for summer, why would you want to work for free? That's the million-dollar question! However, if you look at the big picture, you may find that working for free could actually help you in the long run.

Exploring Possible Careers

Working as a volunteer or an intern at a business is an ideal way to "see inside" a potential career. What a job looks like on the outside may not be what it feels like on the inside. Just because the job looks interesting doesn't mean that it is something that you would want to do day in and day out for years. There have been plenty of students who graduated from college only to find that they didn't actually like working in the profession they had studied.

An internship or volunteer position can help you "test the fit" of a possible career. You can work in a potential career and "try it on" for a short period of time. You can

By working as an intern or volunteer, you can learn new skills. You can also try out a potential career and see if it is what you want to do when you are older.

see if you really want to do this job for a living when you grow up. Not everything that you like needs to be something that you do for a living. Some things are just interesting to try on the weekend or as a hobby.

In high school, the best thing to do is to volunteer in your community. It will fulfill your service learning hours requirement and give you a taste of a possible career.

A Dozen Jobs?

Did you know that most adults today will have twelve jobs during their lifetime? The days of having one job for your entire life are over. One reason is the changing job market. Some jobs disappear because the company moves that job somewhere else in the world. Other jobs are eliminated because they have become outdated. The service or product that job created is no longer needed.

The second reason for job change is personal change. As you grow older, you may want to try new things. Moving to a new area may lead to a career change. Becoming a parent is another reason to change jobs.

Use this to your advantage and try new things. You don't have to do the same thing for the rest of your life. Experiment and try something new.

What Are You Interested In?

With so many possible career choices, how do you know where to start? Which one of those dozen jobs of a lifetime will you try out first? The answer is determined by your interests and abilities.

Spend some time thinking about what you would like to do with your life. Don't think about what your parents or teachers want you to do. This is your life. Think about what you are interested in. If you could live your dream, what would you do? What would you like to try?

There are so many careers that you can try, and everyone is good at something different. Thinking about what you like to do will help you find the best fit.

Do you have a lot of potential career possibilities? Or are you still undecided? It may be that your career path isn't clear to you yet. That's fine. No one said you had to figure out your whole life today. Having a lot of interests can help you with your dozen careers later. Right now, you only have to try out one.

Chapter Two

HOW TO GET AN INTERNSHIP OR A VOLUNTEER OPPORTUNITY

What you already know how to do can help you land a position. Employers want someone who can help them get their work done. What do you already know how to do? What digital skills do you have? What kind of equipment and software programs do you know how to use? Take out a sheet of paper and make a list.

Create a Digital Portfolio

Now that you have a list of your skills, you're ready to create your digital portfolio. With a digital portfolio, you can show everyone your digital skills. Anyone who goes online can see them. Your portfolio can help you find a volunteer position.

At school, your electronic portfolio, also known as an ePortfolio, is used for three different purposes. A working portfolio is for copies of your current work. An assessment portfolio helps you see if you have met your learning goals. A display portfolio is a collection of your best work.

For an internship or volunteer opportunity, a display portfolio is best. You want the world to see only your best work. Select ten to twelve items maximum for your portfolio. Ask a teacher or another mentor to help you decide. Choose only your strongest work. Focus on items that show you have the skills an employer could use.

Assemble your portfolio and put it on the school's Web site with your other portfolios. Or use a free blog service, like WordPress, to place your portfolio online.

Putting Your Skills to Use

There are so many ways to help others with your digital skills. Look over these digital careers and see which one is the best fit for you right now. Which one interests you the most?

Volunteer to Be a Graphic Designer

You can volunteer to work as a graphic designer for a high school club or a local charity. There is always a new fund-raiser that needs advertising materials. Someone has to create the logo, select the type, lay out the text, and design the flyers and the program. Working as a graphic designer close to home will give you items to add to your portfolio year-round.

If you can design Web pages, there are many local organizations that would love to have you volunteer for them. You can create

Showcasing your work in an electronic portfolio will help others see what you can
do. Choose ten to twelve of your best pieces and share your photo, too.

a new Web page or update an old one. Use your skills to help your high school clubs and local nonprofits tell their stories. This will help them reach out to the community and help you build your portfolio.

Volunteer to Be a Photojournalist

Bring your camera when you go to events at your high school and share your pictures afterward. Make it official and run for the position of historian in one of your school clubs. Work for the school newspaper and learn how to meet regular deadlines. Start building your portfolio now.

Working as a graphic designer for a community group can give you practical experience. It will also give you work to add to your portfolio.

Volunteer to be a photojournalist in your community. Take your camera with you to church and sporting events. Send your photos to your local newspaper or TV station so that it can share them with its audience. The more you practice, the more you can develop your skills...and your portfolio.

Protect Your Online Reputation

Before you look for a position, check your online presence. Sign out of all of your social networks. Then type your name into each of the major search engines and see what the public can see. Remove anything that could keep you from enjoying a new opportunity. You want the world to see you as a hard worker, not a hard partier. Some things need to be kept private, so take steps to make that happen and protect your online reputation. If you can't remove the items yourself, contact the Webmaster of each site and ask to have the items removed. Wait a week and then check again. If the changes aren't visible in the search engine yet, write to the search engine help desk and request the removal of their cached pages. Wait another week and follow up if necessary.

Volunteer to Be a Camera Operator

Make videos for your high school clubs and sports teams. Be the go-to person for filming all of your extracurricular activities. School and family events should give you plenty of practice

Practice makes perfect! If you can operate a camera, there will always be something going on at school and in your community that you can film.

filming with your camera and editing on your computer. Write and produce your own short films. You can even create your own YouTube channel.

Volunteer to Be a Social Media Manager

Share all the latest news for your high school clubs as their social media manager. Volunteer your services for one of the many organizations in your local area. Everyone has news they want to share, so use this opportunity to get some volunteer experience.

Volunteer to Do Tech Support

If the word is out that you can fix things, you probably already have a line at your door when something breaks. You can make it official by volunteering your tech support services to local community groups. Charities and nonprofits can always use a helping hand.

Join the Technology Student Association (TSA), a national organization for middle and high school students. This organization has service projects, as well as competitions you can enter and state and national conferences you can attend.

Work with your high school computer club to set up a server, learn a new computer language, or rebuild old computers to give to needy students. Some high school computer clubs provide tech support for both school staff and students. Working with other students is a great way to learn new skills and give back to the community.

Volunteer to Promote Computer Awareness

Today's world runs on computers. Knowing how to fix computers is a valuable skill and one that is in high demand. People everywhere need tech support.

Participate in Computer Science Education Week (CSEdWeek) in December each year. If your school doesn't celebrate this week yet,

17

become an advocate and volunteer to help set it up. Ask your friends at school to help you. Make a video or a poster. Send information about your program to the local media.

Volunteer to Be a Game Tester

Sign up with a gaming company and volunteer to work as a beta tester. It will send you a copy of its new game so that you can play it and send the company feedback. This will give you experience as a tester so that you can see if this is something you want to do later.

Companies always test their new games before they release them to the public. Testing helps the gaming company find any bugs it needs to fix.

Volunteer to Create Your Own Apps

Find a need in your local community and build an app for it. How can you make life at your high school better? How can you help one of your clubs? What can you do for a local charity, church, or nonprofit group? Volunteer your services and help someone else.

Chapter Three

TELLING STORIES WITH WORDS AND PICTURES

For some digital jobs, you help the company tell a story. Graphic designers do this every day when they combine words and images to create printed and electronic materials. Let's look closer at this digital career.

Graphic Designer

Every printed item you see has been designed by someone. Books, greeting cards, billboards, advertisements, and even signs in department stores need someone to design them. As a graphic designer, you will be creating work for a client. The first step is to determine what the client wants. You need to meet with clients to see what they are trying to communicate. Everything in a graphic design sends a message to those who see it. The art, the size of the letters, and the colors that you use in your design all send a message to your intended audience. Each element in your design evokes emotional response. What that message is and what the response will be is determined both by you and your client.

Large or small, every sign you see has been created by a graphic designer. That includes the ones in New York's famous Times Square. Each is designed to send you a message about a product.

You should be prepared to revise your work several times. It can be hard to see what needs to be done without trying it. Meeting with your creative director and/or the client several times is the best way to get the job done. The daily work of a graphic designer involves collaboration.

With so many printed items needed by businesses today, you will have a wide variety of work to do. You could lay out and produce books, magazines, newspapers, journals, and corporate reports. You could create logos for products or businesses. Each company needs a distinctive logo that identifies it and distinguishes it from the rest.

You might be asked to design packaging for a product. Everything that is sold has information on the outside of the bag or the box. Someone has to create the look that the product has when it is sold.

Graphic designers also create all the paperwork that goes with the selling of products. They design the display signs that appear in the stores and the inserts inside of the packages. Yes, someone has to lay out the text for those warranty cards and product manuals in every language imaginable.

If it has words, art, and a design, a graphic designer somewhere created it. With a computer and a variety of software programs, graphic designers tell stories for the companies they work for and bring ideas to life. Needless to say, with all of their work going

Production Design

Most of the work that young graphic designers do is called production design. What this means is that someone else has made all of the decisions. The next step is to make those decisions come to life. What you need to do to make that happen is clearly explained; you just have to sit down and do it. For example, you could be asked to change the language in a product manual from French to Spanish. Or you could work as a letterer and add the words to a comic book. In both of these situations, you are not writing the words yourself, you're adding them to a product that someone else created.

into a computer, storage space is important. If your work is lost because of a computer malfunction, it's gone forever. An external backup drive is a must. Many designers also use the cloud to back up their work. Computers wear out, so duplication is very important.

Instead of moving a computer mouse on a mouse pad, or a finger on a laptop touchpad, graphic designers move an electronic pen on a tablet. The tablet acts like a large drawing pad. What you draw on the tablet appears on the computer monitor. Some advanced tablets act as computer monitors. These large tablets tilt like an art desk so you can skip the mouse pad step and use your electronic pen to draw directly on the screen.

College Internships

When you attend college to study graphic design, you can work as an intern in one of the many areas of graphic design. Every company that creates a product or a service needs graphic design. Many large companies do their own graphic design in-house, so you would be able to intern there and get some practical experience.

When you use an electronic pen and tablet, what you draw on the tablet appears on the computer monitor. You can even use a special pen as a mouse for your computer.

You could also work in a small design studio or a large advertising agency. These are the two places clients come to have their design needs met. Working there would expose you to a wide variety of design projects and give you practical experience in the field.

Professional Organizations

When you enter college, you can join AIGA, the professional association for design. AIGA, formerly known as the American Institute of Graphic Arts, is very active at the college level, so look for the student chapter at your school. You can enroll as a design student for four years at a reduced rate. You can post your portfolio in the AIGA Member Gallery and network at local and national AIGA events. AIGA can help you find internships when you are in school and, later, a job as a graphic designer.

Electronic Graphic Designers

Graphic designers don't just create print images. They also work in electronic media. A motion designer creates the credits for the television shows and movies that you watch. A designer selects a typeface that matches the mood the director wants to convey. All of the text is assembled and put in logical order so that everyone gets credit for what they do. When the show is ready to be sold on a DVD, the designer creates the menu screen text and animation.

Graphic designers work in other electronic media, too. Now that every company has a Web site, they need someone to design it for them. A Web site designer wears many hats. Web site design involves creating both the look of a site and the organization of its content. Unlike a book with a story to follow and pages to turn, most Internet users don't read a Web site from beginning to end. Readers look for keywords and click on them to find the content they want. Then they leave.

A Web page designer needs to make it easy for readers to find the content they want. Decisions have to be made about how to organize the content with both the reader and the Web site owner in mind. What is the company's mission and message? What colors portray the company image? What kinds of photos, illustrations, or videos does the company want to share? What kind of content does the company want to display? Meeting with your creative director or your client will help you figure this out.

The computer language you use depends on the needs of the client. The most basic Web page has HTML (hypertext markup language) with a CSS template. CSS, or cascading style sheets, set up the look of the page step by step. They let you determine the size and color of the type on different locations of the page, like the header, menu, sidebar, body, and footer.

There are many other computer languages used to create Web sites, such as Java, PHP, and ASP, and what is in style is always changing. Flash, for example, was considered a "must" for many years but has fallen out of favor as the Web has gone mobile. Sites with Flash won't display their content on some cell phones and tablets.

After you have created the pages, you need to upload them using FTP, file transfer protocol. Then you can test the pages and share them with the client. Sites are always changing, so Web design can be an ongoing job. Some clients want to change the look of the site at regular intervals, while others simply want you to add updated content. There is always something new to share.

College Internships

Companies everywhere would love to have you intern as a Web designer. Web pages are the public face of companies in every field of business, so there is always a demand. Company sites are always changing and someone needs to update them. If you

Every product needs someone to tell its story. Web pages and print materials help companies share their stories with the public. So do videos. Could one of these jobs be yours?

have motion graphic skills, you could intern at a media company and work on TV credits or commercials.

Professional Organizations

If you want to create Web sites, the World Organization of Webmasters (WOW) is a professional nonprofit organization you can join as a student. WOW works with high schools, community colleges, and universities as well as corporate clients. It links to Web development conferences you can attend and sponsors a jobs board with listings online and on Twitter.

If you want to work with motion graphics, join ACM SIGGRAPH, the Association for Computing Machinery's Special Interest Group on Computer Graphics and Interactive Techniques. SIGGRAPH's parent organization is the Association for Computing Machinery (ACM), the world's first and largest computing society.

SIGGRAPH has an annual five-day conference. It hosts the international SIGGRAPH Computer Animation Festival, showcasing the work of digital film and video creators. This festival is an official qualifying event for the Academy of Motion Picture Arts and Sciences Best Animated Short Film award.

The SIGGRAPH conference has a student volunteer program that includes free full admission to the event. High school students who are eighteen years old qualify for this summer program. If you agree to work thirty hours, you may qualify for a travel assistance award and have your travel costs reimbursed after the event.

Chapter Four

TELLING STORIES WITH A DIGITAL CAMERA

If you know how to use a digital camera, you could turn this skill into a career. Workers in the news and entertainment industries use digital cameras to tell a story. Some stories are about real events, while others are pure imagination. See what it takes to work in these highly competitive jobs.

Photojournalist

Photojournalists use words and pictures to tell a story. They work for TV stations, newspapers, and magazines. Unlike other photographers who work with people who come to their studio, a photojournalist is out in the world looking for stories to share. You need to like working with people to be a photojournalist because that's what you'll be doing—working with people to tell their stories. You can find stories close to home or you can travel the world to find your stories.

Your equipment is a very important part of your job. In years past, the camera was only the first step to telling a story. After the film was developed, it had to be edited before it could be shared. Nowadays the photographs are stored

Photojournalists work out in the field. They go where the stories are, whether that is close to home or on the other side of the globe.

on a small computer disk inside your camera. You can begin editing your photographs on your camera or transfer them to a computer to edit with a software program.

Staying True to the Story

The photographer is expected to capture the story images and edit them. Now you can send your photographs to your editor directly, without relying on anyone else. This ability is a double-edged sword. On one hand, it makes things quite easy for you because you don't have to wait around for anyone else. On the other hand, the software makes it very easy to manipulate the image and make it look like something else. We know this because "doctored" photos are eventually proven false. Now that anyone can take pictures with a cell phone, it is quite easy to catch a lie. The best policy is to tell the truth with your camera. Stay true to the story.

College Internships

When you are in college, you may be able to find a photojournalist internship. Large media companies like to work with college students. Some prefer to work with college students during the summer when you can work for them full-time for several months.

After you have learned the basics in a summer internship, you may be able to find a photojournalist internship during the school year. You would be asked to look for stories just a few hours a week. Having a regular deadline is a good way to keep your skills sharp and develop your portfolio. It is also a good way to get a hold in the marketplace. Some companies hire their interns to work full-time in a paid position after they graduate from college.

Professional Organizations

When you begin studying at the university, make sure that you join NPPA, the National Press Photographers Association. This leading association of photojournalists supports student members in many ways.

If you like to photograph sports, you may also wish to join SEP, the Society of Sports and Event Photographers. This is a different type of storytelling but one that many photographers are interested in.

Videographers

You have probably filmed an event for your family or one of your sports teams. A videographer does this for a living and films special events like weddings, too. After the event is over, the videographer edits the footage and creates a video of the event that attendees can purchase.

Short videos on the Web are also created by videographers. Training videos explain how to do something. Music videos share a song. Professional videographers film music videos for performing artists. Videographers who use music from other performers in their videos always get permission to use that music.

Paying for permission up front is not only the ethical thing to do; it saves time, money, and your reputation. Who wants to work with a so-called professional who is always getting sued for bad behavior? That's not professional at all.

Television, Video, and Motion Picture Camera Operators and Editors

Moving pictures tell a story in a way that stills cannot. Still photographs capture a moment in time. Moving pictures tell a longer story, one that viewers can relive time and again. With the invention of smaller and smaller cameras, the ability to capture motion is now available to almost everyone. If you have a cell phone, you can probably take short movies with it. You can be a camera operator, too.

Professional camera operators can shoot footage with a cell phone, too, but for their work they use more sophisticated cameras. The cameras used for videos, television, and motion pictures are usually much larger than a cell phone, and they film in different formats.

Television camera operators help create every show you see on television. Some travel around the world to capture stories. Others work in a studio all day filming actors for your favorite show. Studio camera operators work with cameras that stay in one place. The camera position is fixed. News camera operators, also called electronic news-gathering (ENG) operators, take their cameras with them.

Camera operators use many different types of cameras to capture a story. Out on assignment, the camera operator is responsible for both the images and the sound.

Once they are on location, they must find the best spot to film the story. Depending on the location, the camera operator will either use a tripod to hold the camera in a fixed position, or carry the camera, using a stabilizer to keep the camera steady.

After the film is taken, it must be sent back to the station for broadcast. The news van is one way to send it. A large pole is erected into the air, carrying the signal back to the station via satellite. Some stations are now using "backpack live transmission." The camera operator wears a backpack with a wireless modem unit inside. This allows the camera operator to send live video and audio feeds while walking in a crowd.

Movies are another place that camera operators and editors work. For the movies, both fixed and handheld cameras with tripods are used. The film director has a big say in how a movie is filmed, so camera operators and film editors work closely with the director each day. For most movies, there is a film crew with several members, and each person has a specific job.

College Internships

You can begin to work in the entertainment industry while you are in college. Television stations and companies in the entertainment business all need interns to help them with their work. Some companies like you to work a few hours a week for the entire school semester. Other internships need you to be available for only a few days during a special event.

At the television station, the camera operator works behind the scenes with a producer and a director. Making the talent look good on camera is part of the job.

Depending on the internship, you could be working as the weekend studio camera operator at a local television station, producing videos for an emerging record producer, or working at an annual industry event for entertainment professionals. There is always something new and exciting happening in the news and entertainment industries.

Professional Organizations

If you want to work in the entertainment industry, you may also need to belong to a labor union. A labor union is an organized group of workers in the same trade or profession that join together to protect their rights. If you work with cameras in the entertainment industry, these are the unions you need to know. The IATSE is the International Alliance of Theatrical Stage Employees, Moving Picture Technicians, Artists and Allied Crafts of the United States, Its Territories and Canada. The International Cinematographers Guild is an organization within the IATSE.

For professionals who work in television broadcasting, there is also the National Association of Broadcast Employees and Technicians–Communications Workers of America. NABET-CWA is a union for workers in the broadcasting, distributing, telecasting, recording, cable, video, sound recording, and related industries in North America.

Chapter Five

DIGITAL PUBLIC RELATIONS CAREERS

When you work in public relations, you are the face of the company. In this digital age, not everyone who does business with a company meets a representative face-to-face. It is quite common to do business digitally, either online or over the phone. In this chapter, we'll be looking at two digital careers you might like to try: social media marketing and call center tech support.

Social Media

More and more companies are hiring someone just to handle their social media. This new type of customer relations requires that someone be online representing the company all day. Depending on how the company is structured, you will work either in marketing and sales, public relations, or the human resources department.

When you work in social media, you are communicating with consumers. Companies want to interact with their customers, and they need someone who can do that rapidly. Now that everyone has access to social media, it is very

A social media manager spends the day online, interacting with customers. Finding out what customers say about the company is an important part of this job.

easy for an unhappy customer to share a bad experience. If a company doesn't act quickly, it will look as if it doesn't care about its customers.

As the social media manager, it will be your job to make sure that you keep track of what consumers are saying about your company. You will need to get in touch with consumers right away to try and help them solve the problem. You don't have to do all of it by yourself, but you do need to be the contact person between the unhappy customer and the person at your company who can help the customer solve his or her problem.

Companies also hire social media managers to spread good news about their company. They want to let customers know about their new products. They want someone to engage with their customers so that their customers become followers or fans. If your company is having some sort of promotional giveaway, it can use social media to spread the news about it.

Customers will come to you if they think that your company can help them meet their needs, so many companies also use social media to send out information about their field. For example, a company that works in health care could send out information about new developments in health care. Sharing this information helps establish the company as an expert in its area of expertise.

As a social media and marketing person you will be responsible for postings to Facebook, Twitter, and the company blog. You may be asked to write this material or the company may want you to gather the material from different areas of the company for posting.

Social media is always changing, so it will be your job to keep up with those changes. As the trends change, you'll need to let your company know what is developing in social media. Your company needs to go where the customers are, and it will be your job to take them there.

College Internships

Social media internships are ideal for college students. Companies want to hire you to use your social media expertise. Some offer college credit for their internships. Because everyone is using social media now, you can look for an internship in a field you are studying. While you use your social networking skills, you can also see what it is like to work in that field. The contacts you make during your internship can help you get a full-time job later.

Professional Organizations

One way for you to meet other social media professionals is to attend their professional networking events. These face-to-face meetings

Social media events, like Social Media Week, take place online and in person all around the world. Professionals attend these events to network with their peers. You can attend, too.

can help you build your professional network and get to know possible mentors.

Social Media World Forum (SMWF) is held each year in London and New York. Social Media Week (SMW) is held simultaneously in a dozen cities around the world twice a year. Different cities act as hosts each time, and most events are free. You could also attend annual blogging conventions, such as BlogWorld & New Media Expo, BlogHer, or BlogWell.

If you don't live in a large city and can't travel out of town for a networking event, you can meet other social media types in your area using a free service called Meetup. Check the Meetup Web site to see who is hosting a social media group near you.

Tech Support

Are you good at fixing things? Perhaps a tech support job is for you. You can have a career helping individuals and companies to keep their computers running. You could work in a call center and

Social Media Is Social

The most important thing about social media is to make it social. That may seem obvious, but you need to be acting as if you are a real person, not a robot. You don't want just to send out messages about how wonderful the company is. That's not very interesting. The most successful social media managers are people who are personable. In other words, they don't just brag about the company, they answer questions and help others.

help customers who call in. Some companies also have chat or e-mail tech support options.

Your job as a tech support person is helping the customers troubleshoot their computer, telephone, Internet, or cable television problem. To do this, you ask the customer a series of questions. What you do next depends on what the answer is.

Some tech support work is based at the company that manufactures the product. Tech support is also provided at companies that use computers to provide a service, such as telephone, Internet, or cable television.

Communication skills are very important in any tech support job. People call the help desk when they can't get their machines to work by themselves. By the time they call you, many customers are already very frustrated. You must be able to listen carefully as they describe their situation and answer your questions so that you can diagnose the problem. Proceeding logically, step-by-step is the best approach. Patience goes a long way in this job. It can also help your customers calm down as they work with you to fix the problem.

College Internships

Some computer manufacturers, like Dell, offer college internships. Apple's customer support group, called AppleCare, actively recruits college students. The AppleCare college pr gram is an internship that lasts the entire school year. The four weeks of full-time training (in your home office) begins in July. You will work from home, and Apple will pay you a salary. Apple will also provide a company phone and computer for you to use, as well as a monthly reimbursement for some of your phone and Internet costs.In return, you work for the company to help customers solve their problems, even on busy weekends and during the holidays when people are home using their computers.

A humanoid robot plays soccer at an International IEEE Conference in Shanghai. Networking with other students at events like these is a valuable way to build connections for your career.

Professional Organizations

College students can join IEEE, "the world's largest professional association dedicated to advancing technological innovation and excellence for the benefit of humanity." IEEE, pronounced "Eye-triple-E," stands for the Institute of Electrical and Electronics Engineers. Student membership is open to individuals studying in the IEEE fields of engineering, computer sciences and information technology, physical sciences, biological and medical sciences, mathematics, technical communications, education, management, law, and policy. One of the benefits of student membership is the Microsoft software that is available at no cost to all active IEEE student members and graduate student members. There are also IEEE student grants as well as access to IEEE's many publications, online courses, conferences, and professional networking events.

Chapter Six

INFORMATION TECHNOLOGY CAREERS

ompanies everywhere work with computers. They need someone to work with the computer hardware, the machines themselves. They also need people who can work with software. If you like to work with computers, this could be the right place for you. Let's look at two careers in this field: business systems and programming.

Business Systems

Businesses also need tech support inside their own company. This is handled by IT, the information technology department. The IT department keeps the servers running and all of the machines on-site working.

You could work at the help desk answering questions that come in from other departments in your company. As a first step, you would try to solve the technical problems over the phone or with e-mail or chat. If that didn't resolve the problem, you would go and work on the computer or server yourself.

The work that you will do in the IT department keeps the rest of the company up and running. Every company needs someone to keep the computers working properly.

Some larger companies outsource their IT departments and hire other companies to handle their tech support. When you work for a third-party tech support organization, you travel from company to company taking care of their hardware, software, and computer system problems. You may visit the same clients on a regular basis throughout the year to check the status of their equipment and perform any maintenance that is needed. The client may also have you on-call, so you visit whenever there is a problem.

College Internships

Now that most companies use computers to conduct their everyday business, there is a high demand for IT workers. When you are in college, you could work as an IT intern in a company of any size in almost any field. Small local companies need IT support and so do large multinational corporations. Computer equipment doesn't last forever, and the more equipment a company has, the more it needs IT support. You may need to undo simple user errors or deal with viruses and other threats from hackers. There is always a need for someone to be on-site to oversee the systems that keep the business running.

```
cellspacing=0 cellpadding"10 borde

ent -->
an="3" bgcolor=#ff9900 widt
' background="../../gifs/bkchrm.gif"
l" size=2>

.n.htm"><b>Back to Home</b></a>
Best html coding by author<br>

= "JavaScript">

ddFavorite(location.href,documen
ookmark this Page</b></A>")
```

Underneath every Web page and inside every program is the code that tells the computer what to do. This code is written in different programming languages.

Professional Organizations

You don't have to wait until you're in college to join a professional organization for information technology. AITP, the Association of Information Technology Professionals, has chapters for high school students, too. If you don't have a chapter in your area, AITP can help you start one. You need to have ten members, some of whom agree to be officers.

AITP can also help you pay for college. It has several college scholarship programs for members. Some scholarships are for high school students who will be attending college in the coming year. There are also several scholarships for student members who are already in college.

Programmer

A computer programmer takes the information that a software engineer has created and makes it into something that the computer can read. This is done by translating all of the information into a programming language, called code.

Today the most common programming languages are C++ and Python. Other programming languages include Java, Perl, PHP, SQL, and Ruby.

Nowadays you can use computer software to help you write code. Yes, you can write a script to help you get the work done. You can write a new script or adapt an old one. Automating some of the routine coding steps will help you get the simplest tasks done more quickly so that you can focus on the more complicated (and more interesting) ones.

If you work at a company that is creating a large software program, it will probably use computer-assisted software engineering, also known as CASE. Just like a script that you can write yourself, computer-assisted software will help you automate parts

IT College Conferences,
Certification, and Competitions

AITP, the Association of Information Technology Professionals, hosts a conference for its college chapters each year. The AITP National Collegiate Conference is a four-day event that includes networking with social events and committee meetings. There are also breakout sessions and workshops about career-related topics and professional exams. After attending the study sessions, you can take two Microsoft exams, the MTA (Microsoft Technology Associate) or the MOS (Microsoft Office Specialist).

Another important professional exam, the ICCP exam, is administered at the conference. ICCP is the Institute for the Certification of Computing Professionals. The ICCP exam is an internationally recognized certification program for the IT profession.

Competitions and scholarships are also part of the National Collegiate Conference (NCC). Throughout the event, teams from college chapters across the nation compete for cash prizes in sixteen different IT categories. The winners are honored at the awards banquet event on Saturday night. On Saturday afternoon, the AITP scholarship winners are announced during a luncheon. Some of the companies that exhibit at NCC also conduct job interviews during the event. There is a lot you can do for your future career in one weekend.

of the coding process. The bigger the program is, the more work there is to be done.

At a company working on a large project, you will work with many programmers to create a new program for consumers or businesses to use. If you like bringing programs to life, working as a programmer can be very satisfying.

Of course, everything that you write has to be tested, and that is the next step in any computer programmer's job. When the code doesn't work, it's pretty obvious right away. Figuring out why it doesn't work and how to fix it is the next challenge. Working step-by-step in a patient manner is best.

College Internships

If you know how to write code in different computer languages, there are many companies who would like to work with you when you are in college. While an internship may not pay you any money, what you gain in experience can be invaluable. You could work as a software tester or spend time programming new projects. You don't have to live near a major software company to find work. Because so many companies use computers now, you could work with a company that specializes in intellectual property or write programs for a music database. The sky is the limit.

Professional Organizations

Two organizations sponsor programming competitions for high school students. The International Olympiad in Informatics (IOI) was started by the United Nations

This Google software engineer is hard at work. A computer programmer takes the information that a software engineer creates and makes it into something the computer can read. Could this be the job for you?

Educational, Scientific and Cultural Organization (UNESCO). During the school year, there are six Web-based contests. A proctored exam follows in the spring. Sixteen students are then invited to training camp during the summer. At the end of this camp, the top four students are selected to represent the United States in the International Olympiad in Informatics. The IOI competition is held in a different country each summer.

SkillsUSA also offers you an opportunity to showcase your computer programming skills. This national nonprofit organization for high school and college students hosts many different types of competitions, including one for computer programming. During the competition, each contestant will receive a packet that includes instructions for writing code for two different projects. Visual Basic, Java, C#, C++ and RPG are the computer languages that are used for this competition.

Chapter Seven

FUN WITH COMPUTERS

Computers aren't just used for work. Many people use computers to play. Maybe you can have a career combining the two. Let's look at what it takes to make apps and games that work on computers and other mobile devices like tablets and phones.

Game Tester

Computer games need to be tested before they are released to the public. Yes, they pay people to play games all day. You will play games over and over and over for hours at a time. The people who do the testing of the games are called testers.

Testing is usually the last step in developing a game. Testing is done at the very end of a project, right before the game is sold to the public. What this means is that anything that is not working properly in the game needs to be fixed. These glitches are called bugs. It is the tester's job to find these bugs and report them

This might sound simple, but you have to realize that testers need to think about every possible thing that a consumer could do with the game. This means that you might have to try something that you would never really do in a game, like drive a car backward.

The testing phase of the game is often a short period of time, typically three or four months. During the testing time, it is common for testers to work seventy or eighty hours in one week. When you consider that most other jobs have a forty-hour workweek, this means that you will be working twice as long as your parents are during any given week. Frankly, it's exhausting. But if you want to work your way up in the video game industry, this is the place to start. Almost everyone begins as a tester.

The Games Publisher Web site lists seventy-three game publishers in North America alone. There are many others spread around the globe. Every game that you play has to be created by someone, and with so many companies here in the United States, there are opportunities to be found.

If you live near a game company, you're in luck! There are always games that need to be tested. Not every job is advertised, so the pros recommend that you send in your résumé when you're ready to work.

College Internships

When you are in college, you may be able to work as an intern at a game company. There are colleges and universities that teach gaming as an academic program now, so these schools have contacts with local video game companies. It's a win-win relationship for both of them. The school can help you get an internship at a game company, and the game company gets the benefit of your school training.

Professional Organizations

When you start attending college, you are also eligible to join the International Game Developers Association. The IGDA is the largest nonprofit membership organization for individuals who

You can learn how to create computer games in college. Yes, there are colleges and universities that teach gaming as an academic program. They work closely with video game companies.

create video games. The IGDA offers student memberships at a reduced rate. College, university, and technical school students with a valid student ID can join as student members and gain access to all of the benefits of regular membership. The only difference is that students are not allowed to vote.

You don't have to wait until college to see what the IGDA has to offer. You can visit its Web site and read all about the game industry. You can also follow IGDA on Twitter, Facebook, and YouTube.

App Developer

Apps are everywhere now, on computers, tablets, and phones. Are you ready to help develop a new product? Apple, the company that created the Macintosh computer, the iPhone, and the iPad, has made it easy for you. Apple has a store where you can sell your product, so it also supports the creation of these new products. In fact, Apple has an entire Web site dedicated to developing applications for the Web. It explains explain how to create an app in great detail.

Creating an app is like baking a cake. You need to have all of your ingredients and tools you'll need on

Can you create an app? Now that smartphones and tablets can go online, Web applications are in high demand. There are Web applications for all kinds of products and services.

hand before you start. First, let's start with the kitchen. To create products for Apple, you need to have a Mac computer with an Intel processor.

The next step is to take out your ingredients and put them on the kitchen counter. Make a folder and save a copy of everything you'll need to create your app. Don't forget the code signing certificates. These certificates will authenticate you as an iOS app developer.

Apple recommends that you learn how to create your app by examining the example projects it has on its Web page. In fact, it allows you to use the code from these examples for your own projects. This looking-at-the-cookbook step will help you get a head start.

After you test the sample projects, you're ready to start cooking by yourself. Now you can begin working on your own app. Remember to include cloud storage as you build your app. Keeping your data on a remote Web server is the latest digital trend.

Once your app is built, it's time to taste what you baked. It's time to test it. You can do a test simulation on your Mac with an iOS Simulator app. After you download the simulator from Apple, you can see the iPhone or iPad user interface in a window on your computer. Use your keyboard and mouse to simulate iPhone and iPad actions as you test your own app. The console logs will save all of the details.

The next step is to test your app on the real thing. You can test the app on your own devices, and ask your friends to do the same. You will need to test your app on the device itself and using Wi-Fi. That's how your app will be used after you make it available to the public.

If you want to take the next step and work at a professional level, you can sign up with Apple to be an iOS developer. Apple will provide you with even more tools to debug your app. As part of your yearly fee, you will also have tech support from engineers at Apple.

Your testing doesn't end there, however. As you continue to tweak the code, you may introduce new bugs into the system. Remember to save your work at each step. The other safeguard is to test only one unit at a time. This will keep you from erasing good code and replacing it with bad code.

After you have the code the way you like it, it's time to test it again. Test your app with as many people as possible before you put it up for sale. Ask your friends and classmates to try the app for you. They won't use it the same way that you do, so you will probably encounter new problems that need to be solved. It's better to solve them now, before you put the app out in the world.

You can also create apps for Android devices. All of the steps are exactly the same; it's just that the app works on a different device. (Someday apps may work on any device, but now that is not the case.)

What Do Game Companies and App Developers Want?

When you are ready to apply for a position with a company that is creating games or applications, you need to bring in something that you have made to show it. On the game developers forum gamedev.net, moderator Tom Sloper recommends that you create a small demo to show what you can do.

Tim Closs, chief technology officer at Ideaworks3D in London, elaborates, "Especially in today's app store economy where you can build a Facebook game and put it up yourself, or build an Android app and put it up on Android Market without any cost investment, then we are really looking for people to do that extra step as part of their portfolio."

College Internships

Companies of all types are looking for summer college interns to help develop new apps. You could work for a technology giant, like IBM or TI, and help it develop apps to sell to its customers. Or you could work for a brand name like UPS (package delivery), Hess (oil and gas exploration), or Smucker's (food), and help it develop apps that improve the company's business processes.

Professional Organizations

Rub elbows with the pros on the app developers' Web sites. The Android Developers Web site has tutorials, videos, free downloads, and many forums you can join. Apple has a library of articles and codes, as well as videos you can use at the iOS Dev Center.

Chapter Eight

HOW TO MAKE THE MOST OF YOUR EXPERIENCE

Working as a volunteer or an intern can be a valuable experience. You can build relationships that can help you now and in the future. Here are a few tips to guide you.

Act Like an Adult in the Workplace

Now that you are out in the working world, you are expected to act like an adult. The clothes you wear and the way you act reflect on both you and the organization. Even though you are not being paid, when you are in the workplace you will need to fit in. Dress the part and speak to others with respect. You can be informal and carefree when you are at home or with your friends. When you go to work, you are an adult. Try it on for size and see how you like it. (You may appreciate your free time even more.)

A mentor can help you learn new things. Working with a mentor can also help you grow as a person. Helping others as an intern or a volunteer helps you, too.

Take Time to Build Relationships

The people that you meet when you volunteer can help you learn new skills and grow as a person. The work that you do can lead to new opportunities. Adults who work in the fields you are interested in can give you practical advice. They can also recommend you to others. This is how networking is done. Helping others also helps you.

Working as an intern at a company can also help you build professional relationships. An employer can write a letter of reference for you. This recommendation can help you get into college or find a new internship at another company next year.

Add to Your Portfolio and Résumé

Many internship and volunteer positions are set up to train young people. The company will teach you new skills so that you can do the work. This will help you on the

The Future Is Digital

"The digital space is booming," says Jordan Goldman, CEO of Unigo.com, a college admissions Web site. He recommends that high school students look at their digital skills with an eye on the future. "Look at how the digital space has impacted every part of our lives and try to anticipate a job that's going to move toward the forefront."

What does the future look like for people working in digital media? Goldman predicts, "Over the next ten years there's going to be an explosion of careers." He goes on to say, "So don't just look at it as a hobby when you're in school. Try to gain skills that you can see being put to use in a full-time career."

job now and in the future. Ask for permission to add some of the work you've done to your ePortfolio. Save the contact information, dates you worked, and the skills you learned in a file. You can add them to your résumé and your college application forms later.

Explore Career Options

Pay close attention to every detail of the work you are asked to do. Is this a career you would enjoy later? Is the work satisfying? Can you grow into it?

Make time to talk to the adults at your summer job. Ask them questions about their work. Their experience on the job can help you with your future career.

While you are at work, observe the other jobs in the organization, too. Could one of them be a fit for you in the future? Talk to the other workers in the break room at lunch and ask them about their jobs. The advice these "industry insiders" give is invaluable.

Plan for Next Summer

After your internship or volunteer position ends, think about what you have learned and get ready for next summer. Will you apply for the same position again, or try something new? What skills do you want to work on next? What industry would you like to explore? Your future is in your hands.

Glossary

annual Happening every year.

apprentice A young person studying with an older person to learn a new skill.

conference A meeting of people with a common interest.

duplication The making of a copy of the original.

ethics The recognized rules of conduct for a group or profession.

extracurricular Outside of the regular school curriculum.

footage Motion picture scenes.

internship A program where beginners work at a company for a limited time.

labor union An organized group of workers in the same trade or profession.

moderator A person who monitors conversations in a group.

networking Creating a support system that shares information and services.

nonprofit Not set up to make money.

portfolio A case that holds your work.

reimbursement A payment made for something already spent.

résumé A written account of your qualifications and experience.

simulation A reenactment done as a test.

stabilizer A mechanical device that keeps the camera in a fixed position for filming.

third party An independent group outside of the company.

tripod A three-legged stand that holds a camera.

volunteer A person who works for free.

For More Information

AIGA, the Professional Association for Design
164 Fifth Avenue
New York, NY 10010
(212) 807-1990
Web site: http://www.aiga.org
Formerly known as the American Institute of Graphic Arts, this
organization has chapters for college students.

Association of Information Technology Professionals (AITP)
401 North Michigan Avenue, Suite 2400
Chicago, IL 60611-4267
(800) 224-9371
Web site: http://www.aitp.org
This worldwide society of professionals in information
technology has chapters for college students.

Institute for Certification of Computing Professionals (ICCP)
2400 East Devon Avenue, Suite 281
Des Plaines, IL 60018
(847) 299-4227
Web site: http://iccp.org
The ICCP is an internationally recognized certification
program for professionals in the information,
communications, and technology industries.

Institute of Electrical and Electronics Engineers, IEEE
Computer Society
2001 L Street NW, Suite 700
Washington, DC 20036-4928
(202) 371-0101
Web site: http://www.computer.org

The world's leading membership organization for computing professionals offers publications, standards, certifications, conferences, and more.

International Game Developers Association (IGDA)
19 Mantua Road
Mount Royal, NJ 08061
(856) 423-2990
Web site: http://www.igda.org
This is the largest nonprofit membership organization for individuals who create video games.

National Press Photographers Association (NPPA)
3200 Croasdaile Drive, Suite 306
Durham, NC 27705
(919) 383-7246
Web site: http://www.nppa.org
The NPPA supports students and professionals who work in news photography, video, and multimedia.

SIGGRAPH: Association for Computing Machinery's Special Interest Group on Graphics and Interactive Techniques
2 Penn Plaza, Suite 701
New York, NY 10121-0701
(800) 342-6626
Web site: http://www.siggraph.org
Open to college students, this worldwide organization is a special interest group of the Association for Computing Machinery.

SkillsUSA
14001 SkillsUSA Way
Leesburg, VA 20176

(703) 777-8810
Web site: http://www.skillsusa.org
This national nonprofit organization for high school and
college students hosts many different types of
competitions, including one for computer programming.

Society of Sport and Event Photographers (SEP)
229 Peachtree Street NE, Suite 2200
Atlanta, GA 30303-1608
(877) 427-3778
Web site: http://sepsociety.com
The SEP provides members with both educational and
professional resources.

Technology Student Association (TSA)
1914 Association Drive
Reston, VA 20191
(703) 860-9000
Web site: http://www.tsaweb.org
The TSA is a student organization for middle school and high
school students with team competitions and an honor society.

Web Sites

Due to the changing nature of Internet links, Rosen Publishing
has developed an online list of Web sites related to the sub-
ject of this book. This site is updated regularly. Please use this
link to access the list:

http://www.rosenlinks.com/FID/DIGI

For Further Reading

Airey, David. *Logo Design Love: A Guide to Creating Iconic Brand Identities.* Berkeley, CA: New Riders, 2010.

Berger, Nicholas. *The Klutz Book of Animation: How to Make Your Own Stop Motion Movies.* Palo Alto, CA: Klutz, 2010.

Christen, Carol, and Richard N. Bolles. *What Color Is Your Parachute? For Teens: Discovering Yourself, Defining Your Future.* 2nd ed. New York, NY: Ten Speed Press, 2010.

Cullen, Kristin. *Layout Workbook: A Real-World Guide to Building Pages in Graphic Design.* Beverly, MA: Rockport Publishers, 2007.

Dille, Flint, and John Zuur Platten. *The Ultimate Guide to Video Game Writing and Design.* Los Angeles, CA: Lone Eagle, 2007.

Farrell, Mary E. *Computer Programming for Teens.* Boston, MA: Course Technology, 2007.

Golombisky, Kim, and Rebecca Hagen. *White Space Is Not Your Enemy: A Beginner's Guide to Communicating Visually Through Graphic, Web and Multimedia Design.* Burlington, MA: Focal Press, 2010.

Kelby, Scott. *Scott Kelby's Digital Photography Boxed Set, Volumes 1, 2, and 3.* Berkeley, CA: Peachpit Press, 2009.

Lanier, Troy, and Clay Nichols. *Filmmaking for Teens: Pulling Off Your Shorts.* 2nd ed. Studio City, CA: Michael Wiese Productions, 2010.

McShaffry, Mike. *Game Coding Complete.* 3rd ed. Boston, MA: Course Technology, 2009.

O'Brien, Lisa. *Lights, Camera, Action!: Making Movies and TV from the Inside Out.* Toronto, ON: Maple Tree Press, 2007.

Oleck, Joan. *Graphic Design and Desktop Publishing.* New York, NY: Rosen Publishing, 2010.

Reeves, Diane Lindsey. *Career Ideas for Teens in Information Technology.* Chicago, IL: Ferguson, 2012.

Rogers, Scott. *Level Up!: The Guide to Great Video Game Design.* West Sussex, England: Wiley, 2010.

Sande, Warren, and Carter Sande. *Hello World! Computer Programming for Kids and Other Beginners.* Greenwich, CT: Manning Publications, 2009.

Sethi, Maneesh. *Game Programming for Teens.* 3rd ed. Boston, MA: Course Technology, 2009.

Skog, Jason. *Setting Up the Shot: Photography Volume 1* (Photography for Teens). Minneapolis, MN: Compass Point Books, 2012.

Sweigart, Al. *Invent Your Own Computer Games with Python.* 2nd ed. San Francisco, CA: Albert\Sweigart, 2010.

Weston, Michael R. *Jerry Yang and David Filo: The Founders of Yahoo!* (Internet Career Biographies). New York, NY: Rosen Publishing, 2006.

White, Casey. *Sergey Brin and Larry Page: The Founders of Google* (Internet Career Biographies). New York, NY: Rosen Publishing, 2006.

Bibliography

Apple Inc. "iOS Dev Center." Retrieved January 28, 2012 (http://developer.apple.com/devcenter/ios/index.action).

Apple Inc. "Jobs at Apple." Retrieved January 28, 2012 (http://www.apple.com/jobs/us/students.html).

Bosch, Cedric. "Life as an Intel Intern." Retrieved January 28, 2012 (http://youtu.be/gV85fyZ4yyM).

Closs. Tim. "Tim Closs, CTO at Ideaworks3D in London Talks to Game Careers at Develop in Brighton." Retrieved January 28, 2012 (http://www.mobilegamesjobs.com/careers.asp).

Dean, Brian. "USA Computing Olympiad." Retrieved January 28, 2012 (http://www.usaco.org).

Dell. "Joining from College." Retrieved January 28, 2012 (http://content.dell.com/us/en/corp/joining-from-college).

Department of Computing Science, University of Alberta. "Ross & Verna Tate High School Internship Program." Retrieved January 28, 2012 (http://launch.cs.ualberta.ca/hip).

District of Columbia Department of Human Resources. "The High School Intern Program (HSIP)." Retrieved January 28, 2012 (http://dchr.dc.gov/dcop/cwp/view,A,1222,Q,638977.asp).

DS Interactive, Ltd. "Games Publishers—List of Jobs and Video Game Publishers." Retrieved January 28, 2012 (http://www.gamespublisher.com).

Goldman, Jordan. "Choosing a College Major to Prepare for the Hot Jobs of the Future." *ABC News*. Retrieved January 28, 2012 (http://www.youtube.com/watch?v=zVnEUD26yeA).

Google, Inc. "Android Developers." Retrieved January 28, 2012 (http://developer.android.com/index.htm).

Hess Corporation. "The College Experience." Retrieved January 28, 2012 (http://www.hess.com/careers/collegeexperience.aspx).

Jobs, Steve. "Steve Jobs' 2005 Stanford Commencement Address: 'Your Time Is Limited, So Don't Waste It Living Someone Else's Life'" Retrieved January 28, 2012 (http://www.huffingtonpost.com/2011/10/05/steve-jobs-stanford-commencement-address_n_997301.html).

Lucasfilm. "Lucasfilm Recruiting: Internships." Retrieved January 28, 2012 (http://jobs.lucasfilm.com/internships.html).

Select Business Solutions. "Computer Aided Software Engineering (CASE Tool) Analysis and Design." Retrieved January 28, 2012 (http://www.selectbs.com/analysis-and-design/computer-aided-software-engineering-case-tool).

Sloper, Tom. "Reply to Writing My Own Video Game Engines to Break into the Gaming Industry." Retrieved January 28, 2012 (http://www.gamedev.net/topic/618342-writing-my-own-video-game-engines-to-break-into-the-gaming-industry).

Smithsonian Institution, Office of Fellowships and Internships. "Smithsonian Opportunities for Research and Study 2011–2012." Retrieved January 28, 2012 (http://www.si.edu/ofg/intern.htm).

Stanford University. "Stanford University Digital Media Internships." Retrieved January 28, 2012 (http://digitalinterns.stanford.edu/student-interns.html).

True, Michael. "Starting and Maintaining a Quality Internship Program." Retrieved January 28, 2012 (https://www.rohan.sdsu.edu/~gsph/fieldpractice/sites/starting-maintaining-quality-internship-program.pdf).

U.S. Department of Labor, Bureau of Statistics. "Occupational Outlook Handbook, 2010–11 Edition." Retrieved January 28, 2012 (http://www.bls.gov/oco).

Index

About the Author

Anastasia Suen is the author of more than one hundred books for children and adults. She has taught many grade levels, from kindergarten through college, and she has worked as a children's literature consultant for many years. Suen lives with her family in Plano, Texas.

Photo Credits

Cover, p. 29 leungchopan/Shutterstock.com; cover (cloud) © iStockphoto.com/kertlis; p. 4 iStockphoto/Thinkstock; pp. 8–9, 44 © AP Images; p. 10 Stockbyte/Thinkstock; pp. 12–13 © Kayte Deioma/PhotoEdit; p. 14 © David Young-Wolff/PhotoEdit; pp. 16, 17 Jupiterimages/Comstock/Thinkstock; p. 18 Image Source/ Getty Images; pp. 20–21 Songquan Deng/Shutterstock.com; p. 23 Leah-Anne Thompson/Shutterstock.com; pp. 26–27 Aaron Tam/AFP/Getty Images; p. 29 leungchopan/Shutterstock.com; pp. 32–33 domturner/Shutterstock.com; pp. 34–35 Digital Vision/ Thinkstock; pp. 38–39 Creatas/Thinkstock; pp. 40–41 © Liuxin Wukaix/Xinhua/Zuma Press; p. 47 .shock/Shutterstock.com; pp. 48–49 nasirkhan/Shutterstock.com; pp. 52–53 Boston Globe/ Getty Images; p. 57 Jetta Productions/Lifesize/Thinkstock; pp. 58–59 Peter Macdiarmid/Getty Images; pp. 64–65 © Jim West/ PhotoEdit; p. 67 PhotoAlto/Sigrid Olsson/Getty Images.

Designer: Michael Moy; Editor: Bethany Bryan;
Photo Researcher: Karen Huang

3|14

DATE DUE

PRINTED IN U.S.A.

ADAMS FREE LIBRARY
92 Park Street
Adams, MA 01220-2096
413-743-8345